What Am I Doing In This Grade?

(A Book for Parents about School Readiness)

Written by
LOUISE BATES AMES, PHD.
Associate Director, Gesell Institute

Illustrated by
GRAHAM SALE

Published by
PROGRAMS FOR EDUCATION, INC.
Flemington, New Jersey

*The hero of this book, John is a December birthday boy who started kindergarten at 4 years and 9 months of age and who finally after two years of struggle and failure, is allowed to repeat first grade, starting this repetition when he was 6 years and 9 months old.

Production by Wendy Shore

ISBN0-935493-00-X

FIVE YEARS OLD

How come I'm always falling asleep in school? Maybe I'm not ready for all this. I wasn't even five when I started school this Fall because I didn't have my birthday till December. Most of the kids are older than I am. Maybe I'm just not ready to be in school all day long. I'd really like to be at home with Mom. When I'm home with her she lets me have a nap in the afternoon if I want one.

Why do they make us little kids try to read and write? I like stories, but it's more fun when Mom reads them to me. The teacher says it's easy to tell a B from a D but I always get them all mixed up.

Lunch is hard, too. I can hardly reach the counter. And once I dropped my tray.

A funny thing is that most every morning my stomach hurts somethin' awful and I can't eat my breakfast. And then when the week-end comes and I don't have to go to school I'm OK. One morning when I was really sick to my stomach, Dad said "He can't get away with that!" But then Mom said, "Maybe he really does feel sick to his stomach. Sometimes I do when things make me anxious.

CEREAL

And this is kind of embarrassin' to tell about because I'm not a baby and I've been dry all night ever since I was three. But since I started kindergarten and found out how hard it was I haven't had too many dry nights.

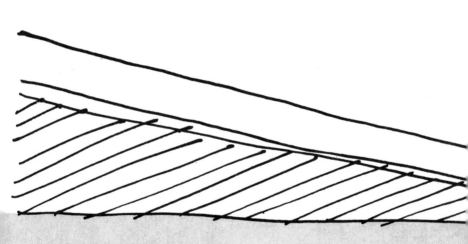

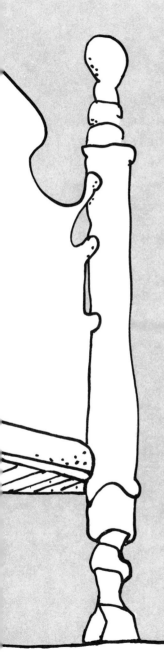

My Grammie came to visit me for my birthday, which was just before Christmas. I can tell Grammie what I really think because she doesn't scold me the way Mom and Dad do. So when she asked me how I liked school I told her I hated it. She sympathized; but I told her not to worry, it was OK. Because I was quittin'. (I didn't really think they would let me; I just wished they would.)

Grammie asked me if I would like to go back to Nursery School because I had liked to be there. I told her the truth: "No chance, Grammie. Once the kindergarten gets hold of you there's no going back."

SIX YEARS OLD

Dad says I've just got to get down to business this year, now that I'm in first grade. And my teacher says I should TRY harder. She says I COULD do the work if only I would try. (The teacher said that last year, too.) My Mom says she thinks it's just the opposite. That I WOULD do it if I COULD.

One day my paper looked so bad
that I just gave up and scribbled
all over it. Boy was I scared then!
The teacher was really mad.

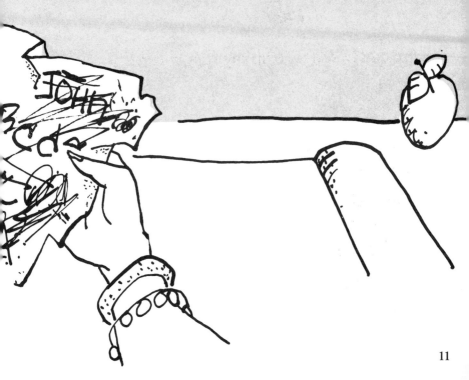

Dad said (last year) that no kid of his was going to flunk kindergarten. Now he says no kid of his is going to flunk first grade so I'd better shape up.

One day I even tore up my report card.

But then they found out and I was really in trouble. They were mad about me tearing it up as well as about my "unacceptable" grades. Now everybody is mad at me.

13

SIX AND A HALF YEARS

Well finally when first grade was almost over, just as I figured there was no way out of this mess and NO HOPE for me at all and that everybody would always be mad at me and I would always be the dumbest kid in the class, my Mom came to my rescue.

Mom persuaded Dad to let her take me to this lady doctor to see if she could help. This lady wasn't like a doctor who makes you well. She was a lady called a Psychologist who knows about children and why they sometimes have such a hard time in school.

She told Mom some complicated things which I didn't exactly understand. It sounded like she was saying that just because a kid was five years old didn't necessarily mean that he would be acting like a five-year-old or would be ready for kindergarten. She said that some boys, and some girls, are just young for their age. (She said that boys mostly develop more slowly than girls. Well I don't know about that!!)

The lady said I might be one of those who was young for my age, and that she could find out by giving me some tests. Well that sounded kind of scary. I thought the tests would be hard.

But they weren't. They were fun. The lady was nice and the tests were easy. I'll tell you about two of the specially easy ones. All I had to do on the first one was copy some things, like a circle and cross and square and triangle. Then a funny one which was a little hard, and a diamond, which the lady said kids of my age couldn't do anyway but she just wanted me to try it.

Then this other one was kind of silly. It was a picture of a person who didn't have all of his parts. So I had to put in the parts that were missing. That was easy.

The lady told me I did just fine; though she said something to Mom about my drawings being a little young for my age and that they had better talk about this.

Anyway after the testing was done the lady talked to Mom a lot. She said that there was no question but that I had been OVERPLACED all along. That is, I started too soon. She said I was clearly young for my age. "Immature" was the word she used. But she said it wasn't bad to be immature and it didn't mean that I was dumb. Just young for my age.

The lady explained to Mom that my teeth were coming in a little more slowly than most and that this, too, was a sign that I was kind of young for my age. She said again that this wasn't bad; just the way I was growing.

The lady said that just the fact that I was a December boy might have meant that I shouldn't have started kindergarten when I did even if I hadn't been a little young for my age. She said that kids tend to do better if they are already five before they start school.

So what the lady advised was that I should RE-PEAT first grade and then things would be easier for me and I would be able to do the work all right and wouldn't get so tired. Whew! What a relief!

Of course when we got home and told Dad, my brother heard them talking and he called me "Dummy." Dad was very helpful. He said to my brother, "No more of that! And I mean it!"

SIX AND A HALF TO SEVEN

When Fall came, and I was in first grade again, none of the other kids said anything.

And when I started bringing home good papers, all correct, even Dad sort of mumbled and said that maybe repeating first grade wasn't such a bad idea after all.

Dad even admitted to Mom that perhaps they should have paid more attention back in kindergarten and first grade when I was having such a hard time.

It used to be so awful in kindergarten. Now it's nice. I really like school.

Anyway I feel pretty good about myself now. I don't want to boast but I think I'm one of the smartest ones in the class. At least the teacher smiles at me a lot, my report cards are OK, and I have fun with the other kids.

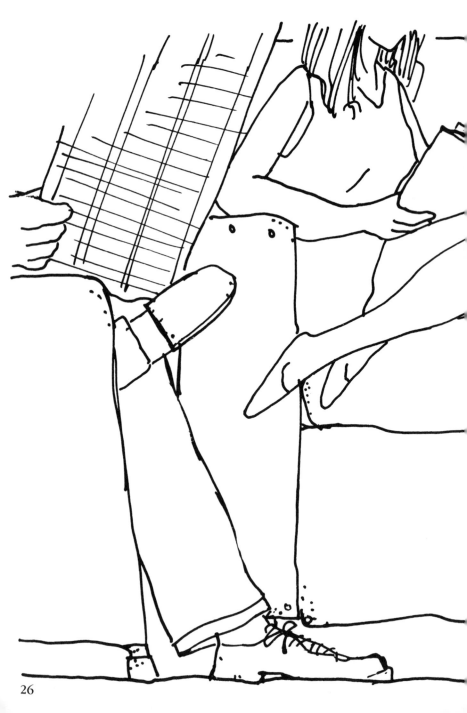

And at home I eat fine now. And that other little problem has gone away, too.

School is really fun now. I never thought I'd be saying that. I always thought school was just a horrible torture they thought up for little kids.

I had no idea my Mom and Dad cared enough about how I felt to go to all that trouble of fixing things up for me. And I'm grateful to that lady, too.